Learning to Read, Step by Step!

Ready to Read   Preschool–Kindergarten
• big type and easy words • rhyme and rhythm • picture clues
For children who know the alphabet and are eager to
begin reading.

Reading with Help   Preschool–Grade 1
• basic vocabulary • short sentences • simple stories
For children who recognize familiar words and sound out
new words with help.

Reading on Your Own   Grades 1–3
• engaging characters • easy-to-follow plots • popular topics
For children who are ready to read on their own.

Reading Paragraphs   Grades 2–3
• challenging vocabulary • short paragraphs • exciting stories
For newly independent readers who read simple sentences
with confidence.

Ready for Chapters   Grades 2–4
• chapters • longer paragraphs • full-color art
For children who want to take the plunge into chapter books
but still like colorful pictures.

STEP INTO READING® is designed to give every child a successful
reading experience. The grade levels are only guides; children will progress
through the steps at their own speed, developing confidence in their reading.
The F&P Text Level on the back cover serves as another tool to help you
choose the right book for your child.

Remember, a lifetime love of reading starts with a single step!

*This book is dedicated to
all the big people who are
helping smaller people
learn to read.
The StoryBots love you!*

Designed by Greg Mako

Copyright © 2019 by StoryBots, Inc.

All rights reserved. Published in the United States by Random House Children's Books, a division of Penguin Random House LLC, New York, and in Canada by Penguin Random House Canada Limited, Toronto.

Step into Reading, Random House, and the Random House colophon are registered trademarks of Penguin Random House LLC.

StoryBots® is a registered trademark of StoryBots, Inc.

Visit us on the Web!
StepIntoReading.com
rhcbooks.com

Educators and librarians, for a variety of teaching tools, visit us at RHTeachersLibrarians.com

ISBN 978-0-525-64613-6 (trade) — ISBN 978-0-525-64614-3 (lib. bdg.) — ISBN 978-0-525-64615-0 (ebook)

Printed in the United States of America
10 9 8

This book has been officially leveled by using the F&P Text Level Gradient™ Leveling System.

TRICERATOPS

by Scott Emmons

illustrated by Nikolas Ilic and Eddie West

Random House 🏠 New York

Some dinosaurs just
fight and fight.

They snap and bite
all day and night!

Triceratops is
not so rough.

He is not mean,
but he is tough!

"Tri" means three—

three horns,
you know.

His horns are not
the kind you blow.

These horns can
help him face a foe.

13

Or else they
help him
get a mate.

Oh, yes,
those horns
are looking great!

His frill may help
protect him, too.

And it looks cool—
that much
is true!

Here are MORE facts
that you should know!

We know that

he is

big and slow.

21

But if a T. rex
comes too near,
Triceratops is
out of here!

He does not like
to hunt for meat.

Plants are what
he likes to eat.

That means he is
a herbivore,

a gentler kind
of dinosaur.

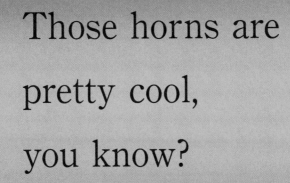

Those horns are
pretty cool,
you know?

No, silly,
NOT the kind
you blow!

29

Showing off his
horns and frill,

Triceratops looks super chill!

Stay cool, Triceratops!